For Today, For Tomorrow

by Lauri Kubuitsile

illustrated by Moni Perez

CAMBRIDGE
UNIVERSITY PRESS

Institute of Education

'This garden is a mess,' Mum said.

'Don't worry, we will tidy it up,'
Hamidi said.

Soon the garden was tidy.

'Here is your pocket money, boys,'
said Mum.

'Now I can buy new crayons,' Beno said.

'I'm saving my money for tomorrow,'
Hamidi said.

The next day, Beno and Omar used the new crayons.

'Look at our pictures, Miss Garcia,' Omar said.

'What beautiful pictures!' Miss Garcia said.

'Look at my picture, Hamidi,' Beno said. 'I used my new crayons. Why don't you buy some, too?'

Hamidi smiled. 'I'm saving my money for something special.'

After school, Beno and Omar bought some ice cream.

'Oh Beno!' said Hamidi. 'You have no more money!'

'What will you use *your* money for?' Beno asked.

Hamidi did not say. He just smiled.

'Let's go to the funfair on Saturday,'
Omar said.

'Oh yes!' Beno said. 'I love the funfair!'

'Do you want to come to the funfair?'
Beno asked.

Hamidi thought about the rides
at the funfair. He loved the carousel.

'Maybe,' Hamidi said.

Hamidi did want to go to the funfair,
but he wanted to save his money, too.
He counted his money.

He had nearly all the money he needed.

No, he would not go to the funfair.
He would save his money.

Hamidi stayed at home.

'Can you help me tidy the sitting room?'
Mum asked.

'Yes, Mum,' said Hamidi.

'I'm home!' Beno said. 'I rode
the orange horse on the carousel.'

'I'm glad you had fun,' Hamidi said.

'Thank you for your help, Hamidi,' Mum said. 'Here is some extra pocket money.'

Hamidi rushed to his room to get his box.

'Where are you going?' Mum called.

'To the shop!' said Hamidi. 'Now I have all the money I need.'

Hamidi ran to the shop.

Mr Maladi was behind the counter smiling. 'So is today the day?' he asked.

Hamidi smiled. 'Yes! I saved my money for today!'

Mr Maladi went to the back of the shop.
He returned with a bright red bike.

'This is for you, Hamidi!' Mr Maladi said.

Omar and Beno watched Hamidi riding his bike.

'Maybe we should save our money,' Beno said.

'Yes, a bike is more fun than crayons and ice cream!' Omar said.

For Today, For Tomorrow ✏ Lauri Kubuitsile

Teaching notes written by Sue Bodman and Glen Franklin

Using this book

Developing reading comprehension

This is a further book in the International School strand of the Cambridge Reading Adventure series featuring Omar and his friends. In this story, Hamidi is saving all his money, but what he is saving for is kept a secret, to both his friends and the reader. This story has an abstract title and teachers will need to explain, linking this to children's own experiences of having to wait for something they really want.

Grammar and sentence structure

- Longer phrases, and more complex sentences with causal connectives such as *'but'* indicating the decisions made by characters.

- Dialogue, indicated by punctuation, is used to move the story forward.

Word meaning and spelling

- Word meanings not directly explained in text, for example: *'carousel'*, *'funfair'*.

- Print features for emphasis, such as the use of italics to stress *'your* money' on page 6.

Curriculum links

PSHE – Thrift and budgeting. Could be linked to the school raising funds to purchase new items through holding a fête, for example.

Maths – How long did it take Hamidi to save up for his bike? How much pocket money did he have? Create different scenarios where children could save money to buy different things.

Learning Outcomes

Children can:

- maintain meaning whilst reading longer, more complex sentences

- self-correct errors on-the-run by cross-checking information from print, meaning, and grammar

- search for and use familiar syllables within words to read longer words

- recognise when information is not overtly explained in the text, and use appropriate inferring strategies.

A guided reading lesson

Book Introduction

Give each child a copy of the book. Read the title and the blurb with them. Remind the children that they have met Beno before. He is Omar's friend. Children could have read some of the earlier International School stories prior to the guided reading lesson. Hamidi is Beno's big brother.

Orientation

Ask the children if they have ever saved up their money for something they really wanted. Have something to share from your own experience.

Give a brief overview of the book:

In this book, Hamidi is saving up to buy something really special. Nobody knows what it is. What do you think it will be?

Let's think about the title: 'For Today, For Tomorrow'. What do you think this means? Draw out the notion that the younger children in the story spend their money as soon as they have it, on things that do not last. By saving his money today, Hamidi has something he can keep for a long time.

Preparation

Move quickly through the book from page 2 to page 6, looking at how Beno and Omar spend their money. Ask: *Did Hamidi tell the boys what he was saving his money for? How do you know? (page 6 – 'Hamidi did not say. He just smiled.') Why do you think he smiled?*

Pages 8 and 9: Here we see that Hamidi has